THE GREATNESS TRILOGY

The Secrets For A Wildly Successful Life

Charles Tchoreret

The Greatness Trilogy: The Secrets For A Wildly Successful Life
Copyright © 2020 Charles Tchoreret

ISBN: 978-1-77277-254-8

All rights reserved. No portion of this book may be reproduced mechanically, electronically, or by any other means, including photocopying, without permission of the publisher or author except in the case of brief quotations embodied in critical articles and reviews. It is illegal to copy this book, post it to a website, or distribute it by any other means without permission from the publisher or author.

Limits of Liability and Disclaimer of Warranty
The author and publisher shall not be liable for your misuse of the enclosed material. This book is strictly for informational and educational purposes only.

Warning – Disclaimer
The purpose of this book is to educate and raise awareness on the Trilogy: Leadership, Fitness and Spirituality as a concept that teaches what it takes to live a wildly successful life. The author and/or publisher do not guarantee that anyone following these techniques, suggestions, tips, ideas, or strategies will become successful. The author and/or publisher shall have neither liability nor responsible to anyone with respect to any loss or damage caused, or alleged to be caused, directly or indirectly by the information contained in this book.

The Greatness Trilogy Disclaimer
The content of this book is provided as an information resource only. It is readers' responsibility to seek professional advice for anything concerning their leadership skills, fitness

Publisher
10-10-10 Publishing
Markham, ON   Canada

Printed in Canada and the United States of America

Table of Contents

Acknowledgments	v
Foreword	vii
Endorsement	ix
Introduction	xi
Chapter 1: Select a Dream To Fulfill	1
Chapter 2: Decide How Great You Want to Be	15
Chapter 3: Take Action	27
Chapter 4: Become a Greatness Fanatic	33
Chapter 5: Seek Spiritual Fulfillment	43
Chapter 6: Live a Life of Service	55
Chapter 7: Get the Support You Need	73
Chapter 8: Never Give Up	85
Conclusion	93

Acknowledgments

I am grateful to my Lord and Savior Jesus Christ for the undeserved grace of becoming an award-winning author, for opening doors, and for the miracles trickling as a result of this amazing experience. All glory to you, Lord.

To my wife Carole, aka Queen C, your love helped me get to this point and cross the finish line. Thank you sweet heart.

To my children, Tryphène, Kevin, Mélissa, and Sally-Jane, for being there. Even when times were difficult, you always had a word of encouragement to lift me up. You all helped me stay focused on the task at hand. Thank you.

What can I say about my grandchildren in Canada: Carla (Carlita), Jayden-Charles (Jay-C), Elena, and Elijah? They did not care much about the important deadlines I had to comply to while writing my book. All they wanted was my undivided attention every time they were around. I'm so grateful for those precious moments engraved in my heart and my memory, which

https://www.charlestchoreret.com/

I will forever keep and cherish. I'm glad I enjoyed every second I spent in their company.

For my other two grandchildren from France: Camille and Loïc, thank you for your messages of love via WhatsApp.

There are countless friends and family members who never stopped encouraging me along the way. Your kind words helped me reach and cross the finish line. Thank you for your support. You are all amazing!

"The prime objective of the Greatness Trilogy concept—Leadership, Fitness, and Spirituality—is to help you unleash the best version of yourself in everything you get involved with, and to raise your awareness that you are solely responsible for who you want to become. The impact you will have on people around you will determine to a large extent how you will be remembered and what your legacy will be."
– Charles Tchoreret

Foreword

Are you living the life you always dreamed of? Are you living your life to the fullest, while at the same time showcasing the best version of yourself in all you do?

The Greatness Trilogy: The Secrets For A Wildly Successful Life is a gift that you can use on your journey toward personal greatness. Author Charles Tchoreret is the founder and owner of The Greatness Trilogy brand, and is dedicated to giving you the keys to the greatest you. The three components of the Trilogy are Leadership, Fitness and Spirituality, and it is these components that will help you be wildly successful in all areas of your life. This is not about you becoming a different person, but rather becoming more of who you are.

As you integrate the Trilogy into your current mode of operation, you will discover how to overcome your current challenges. No matter who you are or what your current situation is, regardless of your age, culture, beliefs or religion, this book is full of insights, and will act as a guide in your personal life, teaching you the steps to take to achieve continuous and lasting greatness.

https://www.charlestchoreret.com/

Charles shares with you all his personal experiences to help you define your purpose as a successful leader, and shows you how to overcome the limitations that may be holding you back. He believes that nothing is big enough to stop you from being successful, provided that you follow the recommendations described in his book. This guide will help you build your character and personality, and help you develop a heart of service, focusing on the needs of people around you as your first priority.

Get ready to learn from this amazing book and create massive change in both your business and personal life, and tap into continuous GREATNESS.

Raymond Aaron
New York Times Bestselling Author

Endorsement

"This powerful book, like its author, is innovative, inspirational, and a bar raiser for those who want the best out of life and greatness from themselves!"

Dr. Ona Brown, Author of *Discover the Greatest YOU!*

Introduction

While working in the corporate world, my understanding of greatness and success were based on criteria set by society, thus deliberately sweeping my own understanding and values under the carpet.

Defining greatness, in general, goes beyond a mere personal perspective. It is a combination of self-positioning and, more importantly, how people see you.

The journey you are about to start, through this book, boils down to incorporating the trilogy: **Leadership**, **Fitness**, and **Spirituality**, as the true reflection of who you are as an individual and game changer.

Over the years, I have discovered that applying leadership, fitness, and spirituality principles in every sphere of my life helped me find balance—the ideal that I needed for lining up the rocks of my life properly. Those rocks are the things I care about, like my core values, my business principles, my customers and students, my children and grandchildren.

This book will show you how you can align your rocks and enjoy your life to the fullest.

Achieving greatness is a personal responsibility. It is your decision. Over the years, I learnt that success is an act of self-love and love for others, and that focusing on just making money is the wrong approach to achieving lasting success on your path to greatness.

This book will help you build your greatness on solid foundations. To weather tests of every day's twists and turns, your ambition must be cemented in your heart with uncompromising conviction. I urge you to find your own conviction, be it through your spirituality, your inner power, your church, your mosque, or nature—whatever that inspiration may be, act on it.

Even if you don't feel that conviction at this point, embark on this journey with an open mind. As you learn how to do that in these pages, focus on the low-hanging fruit. Do those actions or rituals that are easiest to implement right away to get some quick wins, which will increase your conviction and confidence. Take it step by step, small bits by small bits. If you use the fundamental principles of this book to achieve greatness in your life, by aligning your leadership, your fitness, and your spirituality, you will never look back.

Introduction

I invite you to get the most out of this book through three simple stand points:

1. Don't overanalyze

Don't get paralyzed by too much analysis of what you will learn. Have an open mind and commit to educating yourself at your own pace, and implement the recommendations therein offered. This is not a race. This book is a reference manual that you should revisit to consolidate what you have already learnt.

2. Quiet the noise

The most dangerous noises, when it comes to changing your habits and taking yourself to the next level, are those noises coming from within you. We are our own worst enemy. Quiet the inner voices that tell you that you cannot make it.

"We're our own worst enemy. You doubt yourself more than anybody else ever will. If you can get past that, you can be successful."
– Michael Strahan (former American footballer)

3. Focus on the low-hanging fruit

As you embark on this process, focus and enjoy every little step you can take toward making your dream come true. Running a marathon starts with taking the first stride, and as you get momentum, you get more confident for the remainder of the race. Every achievement toward your objective, no matter how small, should be an opportunity for you to celebrate. Be clear on your course of action, and identify those easy-to-implement actions that you will take in order to get yourself to where you want to be.

Remember that I'm teaching you a step-by-step process, especially if you have never considered the trilogy—**Leadership, Fitness,** and **Spirituality**—as being what will help you discover the secrets for a **wildly successful life**. I could never say it enough: The journey to greatness is a marathon, not a sprint. Quick wins are a must because they create confidence, which is the foundation for long-term success. Think about the change management approach that suits you best, and adopt it in a logical fashion by being capable of reasoning in an orderly fashion on the wealth of information you will receive. Remember, this is your journey, and whatever is taught to you must make sense.

Introduction

I presume that you have decided to be on this journey because this is a decision you have consciously made. Therefore, you need to be aware of some prerequisites for any change to take place. They include:

a. **Establish a sense of urgency** on how you can best make a paradigm shift from where you are to where you want to be, in the next one year, three years, or five years.

As you will use the Greatness Trilogy—**Leadership, Fitness,** and **Spirituality**—to define the new you, be accountable to yourself in the way you see this process unfolding; you may need to share your vision with someone who will encourage you on your journey. Take full ownership of this transformational exercise, and enjoy every moment of it.

b. **Create a clear and achievable vision.**

Creating a vision for your life might seem like a frivolous, fantastical waste of time, but it's not. Having a clear vision of the life you want is actually one of the most effective strategies for achieving the life of your dreams. Perhaps the best way to look at the concept of a life vision is as a GPS to help guide you make the right decisions on your way to your final destination. Your vision will propel you toward the life of your dreams.

Definition of the Greatness Trilogy

At this point, I believe that for the sake of clarity, defining the Greatness Trilogy is pivotal to understanding what you are going to learn. Starting with the word "**greatness**," it is often associated with the likes of power, control, and status. It is generally believed that to be great means acquiring a high position in society, to be recognized for the things that you've accomplished, or to be known by many across the entire world. Those are the things that the world keeps preaching to us, but is that what it really means to be great?

The Greatness Trilogy embodies a more simplistic, accessible, inclusive, and an "I can do it" definition, with deeper and more lasting meaning for each individual; whether you are a stay-at-home mom, a blue or white collar worker, or a business executive, the concept will bring you to the realization that "greatness" has nothing to do with your possessions or status. It is more related to your motives. Being great means impacting those around you, adding value to them, not for the sake of self-interest, but out of passion, kindness, and inspiration. When you focus

Introduction

more on your purpose and serving others, the "greatness" that you feel will be much more satisfying than what you receive from simply climbing society's ladder; hence the importance of "spirituality" as one of the three pillars of the Greatness Trilogy concept, as we will see later in the book.

Before getting to that, allow me to define "Trilogy."

The dictionary defines a trilogy as a group or series of three related things. This book is about **Leadership**, **Fitness**, and **Spirituality**; three elements, which when brought together, give you the alignment you need to strive for in your personal life, and also how you can become a game changer in the life of people around you. These three elements combined will help you define who you are and how people see you.

I have always had a special interest in the spiritual meaning of the number three, which represents the trinity: **mind**, **body**, and **spirit**, or the Trinity, **Father**, **Son**, and **the Holy Spirit** as one.

Three (3) is the number of the whole and of completeness. In the context of this project, you have:

- **Leadership:** Embodying taking full responsibility of your life, leading it in the direction that is best for you. When you can take responsibility for yourself, you are better able to have a positive and inspiring impact on others.

No matter what activity you're in, your leadership approach should have one prime consideration: human well-being. Why am I saying this? Well! *"Leadership is not about asserting yourself over somebody. Rather, it is to harness everybody's aspiration and make it happen"* – **Sadhguru.** Good leadership is about knowing how to lead yourself and, ultimately, how to lead others. In your ambition to lead others, you will only be able to give what you know or what you have. If you don't know how to lead yourself, it will be reflected in the way you lead others (i.e. poor leadership). A good leader thinks "we," and not "you" vs "me." A good leader gives an inclusive approach to his leadership style, and because he recognizes that the work he is embarking on is important, he makes sure to improve in every sphere of his life. As we will see later in the book, it does not matter which activity you're in—be it a stay-at-home mom, a head of state, a business professional, or a blue collar or a white collar worker—three basic qualities will set you apart and make you into a leader of first choice:

1. Your integrity;

2. Your ability to inspire others to do the right things;

Introduction

3. Your insight: your ability to have an accurate and deep intuitive understanding of situations.

   This is the level of leadership I'm teaching, bringing you to develop a heart of service as you move from an egocentric perspective to one where others come first.

- **Fitness:** You are privileged to have been beautifully and powerfully created; therefore, it is your responsibility to take care of yourself, both physically and mentally. Let's look at the physical side of fitness. Let me tell you a short story. Once, in a hospital, a junior doctor went to see his senior colleague about the condition of one of his patients. The senior doctor said to him: "Oh! Now he is vomiting, is he?" "Yes," said the junior doctor, "but nothing in the results we have can justify him vomiting." Then the senior doctor said: "Ask him if he plays golf. If he does, ask him to stop, and if he does not, ask him to play, and then he will become okay." This is what it takes to be healthy and fit. Some people add a reasonable level of physical training, three to four times a week, with two to four days of rest in between, and maintain a top physical condition; they are upbeat and ready to impact the world. Whereas others hardly move all day long. They are sluggish, and their body language reveals their inability to be good leaders. You need to have a good balance between time of physical exercise and time of rest. Your body needs both.

A strong body is the vehicle that will take you from A to Z to interact with your audience or your community. A leader's performance requires that they spend a great deal of energy, both physical and mental. Regular exercise is one of the key ways to maintain a healthy and energetic body.

Being physically fit is important, but you also have to be intellectually fit. What do I mean by that? Being a great leader isn't an accomplishment that can be attained by right or through a degree. It is something that has to be earned by those who are really worth it. Regardless of the field that a leader may operate in, it is quite safe to say that their leadership requirements evolve with time. If a leader isn't equipped to handle these requirements or challenges, then they most certainly wouldn't be able to "lead" adequately. As the great leader you are or want to become, are you putting yourself in a continuous learning mode? It is necessary that you renew your skill sets on a daily basis, in order to always be on top of the game and be a leader of first choice. Your audience will have different expectations based on their personal journey, but you should be able to understand where they are coming from, and to guide them accordingly.

Introduction

- **Spirituality** (inner power, values, the Universe, nature, etc., dependent on your personal belief): It is the element that gels everything together; the elevating element that will take you to the next level, shifting your perception from the risk of self-centeredness, to one dedicated to rendering intentional service to others as a priority. Applying scrupulously the Greatness Trilogy concept will bring you success. As you get successful, you may be tempted to think that it's all about you—that's human nature—and that you are pretty special. To stop your ego from taking control of your life, you need a stronger power to keep you grounded and level-headed. This is where the power of spirituality comes into play. I'm talking about spirituality beyond religious, dogmatic connotation, but a power within that will help you have a different insight on your leadership role and not making it the center of your life in a selfish way. As a great leader, you want to be a role model rooted on solid moral principles, values, and integrity.

I'm advocating a paradigm shift, where your inner, God-inspired values will help you become the service provider of first choice, a committed servant to the people you serve, hence becoming conscious that you are accountable to them. **To whom much is given, much is expected.**

Remember, as you embark on this journey, you started from somewhere; you were not born nor chosen into greatness. Some people may believe that we are predestined to be who we are. I don't believe it—to the exception of Jesus Christ as related in the Holy Bible. If some force has already determined your future, then trying to take care of yourself is useless. The idea that God—the Universe—foreknows all decisions, would mean that he is *responsible* for all that happens, including wars, injustices, and suffering. Is that possible? No, your future is not planned out before you, and your own decisions determine what your everlasting future will be. Having said that, you are born with the potential to be great. The Word of God teaches us that God breathed into man the breath of life. Therefore, Divine empowerment was a prerequisite to function as God's image and to be God's vice-regent. God blessed man and woman, and said to them, *"Be fruitful and increase in number; fill the earth and subdue it. Rule over the fish in the sea and the birds in the sky, and over every living creature that moves on the ground."* God never told man to sit back and that He would do everything on man's behalf. God did not create robots. God wanted man to be a reactive and action-driven creature; a creature that makes a difference: an impactful being.

Introduction

When you take the example of people who have impacted this world, you see that they decided to make a change. Such people were icons like Martin Luther King Jr., Nelson Mandela, Mother Teresa, and many others. They were regular boys and girls born in their respective countries, leading their lives like any other kids, to later on become great leaders in their respective fields. They decided to change something in society they were not happy with—an undertaking bigger than themselves and stripped of any selfish aspirations. I think that you have the potential to become great; you just need to remind yourself that you are not living for society's approval, but for your cause, your purpose, and your mission. You choose who you want to become, and you take action accordingly to make it happen.

The next chapters will take the debate to another level, bringing in a dimension that is too often left out or not really emphasized upon, and I will show you why the approach I suggest is pivotal to achieving greatness.

Once you have completed your journey through this book, I'd like you to interact with me. It will be my pleasure to work personally with you on your own itinerary to discover **the secrets to a wildly successful life,** through *The Greatness Trilogy.*

https://www.charlestchoreret.com/

Interact with me on:
my website: www.charlestchoreret.com
Instagram: https://bit.ly/30gQCxk
Facebook: https://bit.ly/3byICvj
YouTube: https://bit.ly/33WSjB7

Enjoy your journey to the discovery and unleashing of the GREATEST YOU!

Chapter 1

Select a Dream to Fulfill

Where and how do you see yourself in the next five, ten, or fifteen years? What are the dreams that you have for your future? Your greatness will start with a dream. Greatness is not something that just happens. It is the result of conscience choice and discipline. What does this mean? Everything under the sun begins with a dream. All those who succeeded in life went the extra mile to put their dream into action. Earlier in this book, I referred to great leaders who impacted the world in a profound way. People like Martin Luther King Jr., Nelson Mandela, and Mother Teresa are good examples of people who decided to commit to their mission. They selected a dream and they fulfilled it. What is remarkable with their achievement is that they committed to something bigger than themselves.

The causes they were fighting for had no selfish motives.

In all my international travels, I realized that no matter where I went in the world, people are generally the same. There are more commonalities than there are differences between people, no matter which country they are from. In every place I have been, people are looking for ways to improve themselves; they are looking for ways to express the best version of themselves. They all have dreams: dreams of a better future, and dreams of a better life for their family and loved ones. Some go even further by having dreams for the improvement of their community or their country. They all are looking for ways to get better. They want the information; they want the knowledge.

I don't know what your dream is. However, my hope is that you will have one that takes you beyond your little self, to a dimension that's bigger than you. It might sound like a scary thought, but that's alright. Ellen Johnson Sirleaf, Africa's first woman president, said in one of her books: **"The size of your dreams must always exceed your current capacity to achieve them. If your dreams don't scare you, they aren't big enough".**

This is for you to understand that dreams are important. Without dreams, there will be no ambitions to chase.

Select a Dream to Fulfill

Having dreams will imply that you have to put them into action. It means that if you are working on a goal or anything you want to achieve, you have to consciously choose to be the best you can be in making it happen. On a daily basis, we can see the outcomes of dreams that have materialized and that are making a fundamental difference in our lives. Having big dreams is very important and, who knows, it might be dreams that change the course of not only your life but the entire world. Big dreams motivate, inspire, improve, and help you in achieving any goal that you want to achieve. It is the most important thing in life, and without dreams, we will be nowhere.

I have no doubt that you have dreams, big or small; most people have dreams. People, past and present, who have made a difference in this humanity, had dreams, and that is what makes them who they are today. Every human being needs to dream and dream BIG. The bigger the dream, the better. A big dream will take you out of your comfort zone and force you to be both resilient and determined to find ways to materialize it.

To have dreams is important, and to deny someone the right to dream, could be considered a crime. Allow me to open a parenthesis. In some countries in the world, people are being denied the right to free elections; thus, the right to ever envisage the materialization of free elections. Children are denied the right to be children; their dreams are destroyed because of forced labor or forced prostitution. Women are being refused the right to dream of freedom, and the list goes on.

Dreaming is essential for a human being. Without dreams, you will lose interest in life and finally hate to live life. You will be bored and tired of the same monotonous routines of your daily life, and will not even find interest in the most exciting things. Only with dreams will you find a purpose to live your life. You will start working hard toward the dream, and you will never lose interest in life. You will never tire and will always be motivated. This is the best way to become successful and, ultimately, to express the greatest version of you, through the power of dreams.

When you look at the world today, what will be your positive contribution to make a difference? It could simply be a difference you'd make within your family, your community, your country, or even the world. What will it be?

As you choose your dream, be realistic and know that with any dream, comes great responsibility. It is just not enough to dream and forget about that dream. Many people dream, but only some wake up and work for it. It is essential to work hard for your dreams. Without this hard work, a dream will only remain a desire in the subconscious mind, and will never be achieved.

I recently launched an initiative, a dream dear to my heart and titled **"AFRICA: A Heaven on Earth Continent."** The project's aim is to trigger a paradigm shift in the way the world pictures Africa, through stereotypes and how Africans see themselves. The objective is to educate the people of Africa, from the grassroots up, on how they can write their new story, in their own words. Those who want to know more about this project can contact me directly.

Dreams allow you to enjoy the luxuries of life or all that life has to offer. Without a dream, you will never feel the accelerated excitement felt through achievement. We get motivated when we achieve things. Without that possibility, we would not feel happiness. Dreaming helps you go beyond your apparent limitations, and forces you to be in constant improvement. Constant improvement helps you adopt an "**I can**" attitude, always pressing forward and always pushing your limitations toward surpassing challenges in your way, by going the extra mile. Fulfilling a dream is very challenging most of the time. Failures may come, but an attitude of commitment and continuous improvement is thoroughly important in order to succeed. Dreams are the fuel that keeps you energized to do even better. Even if there are many obstacles in your transformational process, you will keep moving forward and will try to always dig deeper inside of you.

Following your dream can open the path to the greatest you. It will require some work on your part, and the journey might be intimidating. Like anything in life, it will require sacrifice, in terms of time or even money. This is the point where most people stall. It's a lot of work. You will have to be willing to get into that part of yourself that's actually committed to making a difference and making your dream come true. Oftentimes, we say that we want it, but we are not always ready to pay the price.

My wish for you, as you choose the dream you want to fulfill, is that you can let it be one that reflects your expectations for a cause you are passionate about, and one that will help you be the change maker you are. Until you activate your dream, you are in your comfort zone. Your creativity will be triggered when you step out of your comfort zone. As you do that, you're taking a risk and opening yourself up to the possibility of stress and anxiety. At this point, you're not quite sure what will happen and how you will respond to the pressure. The good news is that you've stepped out of your familiar environment. That's a

Select a Dream to Fulfill

good start; you have decided that there's no turning back. Just like the old adage says, **"If you want to take the island, burn the boats."** When you burn the boats, you have no choice but to work on your dream and change your new reality.

What does it take for you to materialize that dream you have dormant inside of you?

Three key attributes:

1. A compelling dream or vision

You know that it will be a gift once you achieve it.

2. A strong reason to make it happen

Reasons will help you follow through when the going gets tough. It is not an easy ride. Most people know what they want to achieve, but they don't have strong enough reasons to push them through. As a result, they give up on their dreams, and they live a life of regrets as the years go on.

"Cemeteries are full of unfulfilled dreams... countless echoes of 'could have' and 'should have'... Don't choose to walk the well-worn path to regret."
— Steve Maraboli

3. A "why" strong enough to prevent fear from creeping in

Fear is one of the biggest killers of dreams and hopes. Don't allow it into your space. If you don't take action because of fear of failure, you FAIL by default, because you are living a life you do not want to live, a life less than your potential. Failure is NOTHING compared with the feeling of REGRET. I dare you to jump into the deep end of your dream. The worst-case scenario is that you will learn a big lesson from the experience and grow from it. My recommendation: Press forward until you achieve your dream.

There you are, all set. To close this first leg of our journey, I offer you 7 steps you can apply to fulfill your dream.

1. **Select a dream to fulfill**. You may have many dreams swirling in your mind, and you don't know where to start. Choose one dream and take action. Whether the decision is to write a book, run a marathon, buy a home, or find true love, fulfillment always starts with the intentional identification of one single goal and the heartfelt conviction to accomplish it. Take some time. Pick one, and then set out to accomplish it.

Select a Dream to Fulfill

2. ***Believe it is achievable.*** Refuse to be a statistic and be counted among those who will never accomplish their dreams because they simply refuse to believe in themselves. Optimism is absolutely required for dream fulfillment and life enjoyment.

3. ***Support is always good to have.*** People have done it before you. You don't have to reinvent the wheel. Take advantage of their experience, and work on your own dream. When I decided to become an author, I enrolled in the 10-10-10 program, with my coach and mentor, Raymond Aaron, and learned how to write a book. As I got into that space, I realized that there is more to writing a book than just submitting a manuscript. It takes someone to do infographics for the cover and back cover, an editor to ensure that your content complies with writing rules, a catchy and compliant title and subtitle, and a book architect to guide you along the way. You don't have to be alone. If you need help on how to choose a dream to fulfill, it would be my pleasure to collaborate with you.

4. ***Adjust your life as necessary.*** If for some reason you are struggling to accomplish your dream, it could be a sign that you need to adjust your lifestyle accordingly. Some of the adjustments

may be major, but they always start small. In my case, writing a book meant that I had to decide on what I wanted to write about, and give myself the time and space to make it happen. I had to make space for the new me that was shaping up. Your dream may be to run a marathon. Start building yourself up by running one mile. Maybe you want to start going to the gym. A gradual start would be recommended. Don't emulate those who have been training longer than you. Go one step at a time. The first step is always the easiest; the second one will be too.

5. **Set a deadline.** Deadlines force our hand and call us to action. Therefore, it is absolutely essential to pick a realistic timeline and get moving. You don't want your dream to be just a wish.

6. **Tell others.** Share your dream with like-minded people and NEVER with naysayers. As you speak to the right people, you never know where help will come from. A year ago, I attended a workshop in Toronto. On the second day, the guest speaker, Martin Rutter, The founder of "Project Heaven On Earth" asked participants to share a project they were working on and that could potentially make a difference in the lives of others. I decided to share mine. At the time, I was working on my project, The Greatness Trilogy, and trying to figure out how its

Select a Dream to Fulfill

three components—**Leadership, Fitness,** and **Spirituality**—could enhance a paradigm shift in people's lives. The guest speaker shared with us his project, "Heaven On Earth." That was all I needed to hear. I got filled with a sudden surge of inspiration. As a result of that exchange, I have now extended **The Greatness Trilogy**—which embodies leadership, fitness, and spirituality—to my new project, **AFRICA: A Heaven on Earth Continent**. This is simply to emphasize that you never know where help will come from.

7. ***Stay focused and never give up***. Fulfilling your dream will require perseverance. There will be successes and failures along the way. Persevere through those failures, and you will accomplish your dream. Giving up is not an option, unless you want to go back to square #1. Think about it; if you've gotten this far, why would you want to start over? Instead of allowing failure to kill your dream, use it to refocus yourself and your resolve.

"Keep your dreams alive. Understand that to achieve anything requires faith and belief in yourself, vision, hard work, determination, and dedication. Remember, all things are possible for those who believe."
– Gail Devers

There comes a time in life when we need to ask ourselves the right question. You may have dreams; there is something in you that you want to accomplish, but for some reason, you don't seem able to take a stand and make it happen. When you are in that situation, it's time to ask yourself if there is something you need to do to break whichever emotion it is that's stopping you from moving forward.

You may seemingly have everything you need to be content: a good job, a beautiful wife and family; however, sometimes, in your quiet moments, you might find yourself with that uncomfortable, nagging question…

Am I actually happy?

For most people, to avoid thinking about it, they distract themselves with different activities to help them keep their minds off the real issue. One such distraction today is social media.

Maybe you have immersed yourself excessively into your responsibilities as a father, a mother, a spouse, an employee, etc., but deep down, your happiness is still an issue; even though you make well over 6 figures, and you love what you are doing and every privilege that comes with it, you still have no contentment. There is something that you hate about your current situation.

This could be the story of anyone having a successful career. They find themselves wondering, "Is this all there is?" at least once a day.

So what do they do most of the time? Nothing.

Why? Because they are driven by fear. After all, they are responsible adults who followed the path that responsible adults take. They have a solid post-graduate degree, a house, a spouse, and children. They could be the main breadwinner in their family, so they are too afraid to change their situation.

They start building scenarios to justify why they should not fulfill that dream that is dormant in them. There was a good friend of mine who wouldn't dare take a leap of faith because he did not want to be the cause of his family ending up homeless. He was afraid that he might find out that he didn't have what it took to be successful on his own, and he was afraid that he would prove that the naysayers at his firm were right, and be wracked with embarrassment and shame.

My friend was reasoning with himself in an effort to try to feel better. He tried convincing himself that it was not so bad. He told himself that he enjoyed the atmosphere in the office, even though there were questionable things here and there, and that it was not so bad. After all, he thought, isn't this what most people's lives are like? Who was he to want something different?

I have known my friend for over 25 years, and I know that his dream had always been to start his own business.

This internal tug of war went on for over a year until I decided to sit him down and have a serious talk with him. I knew that he could not take it anymore. I told him that he needed to give it a try, and that it was not fair for him to live a life that he did not enjoy.

I wanted him to try and see if his life could expand from okay to great. I encouraged him to consider creating the life that he wanted, instead of just settling for the resigned ennui that so many people around him accept. I needed him to see that he had in him a life that was authentically his.

Believe it or not, after a couple of months, he faced his fears and decided to quit his job and follow his dream. Fifteen years down the line, he is now a successful entrepreneur, and wondering why he did not have faith in himself all those years.

Chapter 2

Decide How Great You Want to Be

Welcome to your onward journey. This second chapter will require you to make a truthful self-assessment.

Now that you have chosen the dream you want to fulfill, I invite you to ponder these two questions: How far do you want to take your dream? How great do you want to be once you accomplish your dream?

At this point, everything is crystal clear; you have understood and applied the 7 steps to fulfill your dream. The dream you have set might be something like being a successful life coach, being an international motivational speaker, writing a book, owning a house, having a certain income, or getting into a certain position professionally. Your dream might be to improve your interpersonal skills through personal development; it might be to improve your physical condition through exercising four times a week, because you know that being fit is a pivotal element of the new person you have decided to become. Whichever the case may be, your dream is about you, and only you can trigger the mechanism to make it happen.

If your dream is crystal clear in your head, with realistic deadlines, which I believe it is, then you already know the role that clarity plays in getting resounding results. As **Yogi Berra** said, *"If you don't know where you are going, you might not get there."* Deciding what you want is critically important to achieving anything. Most people don't even do that, and they end up becoming, as Zig Ziglar says, *"wandering generalities instead of meaningful specifics."*

More Important Than Your Dream

There is a decision you need to make that is more important than the dream you set for yourself; it is who you want to be and how great you want to be. Who you are will define your life far more than the environment you try to create around you. Of the few that set clear goals for their lives, few of them really ask the question, **"Who do I want to be?"**

Deciding who you want to be transcends the personal dream you set for yourself. Setting a dream to improve your fitness, wealth, or any other aspect of your life, is just another **"to have"** goal instead of a

"to be" goal. The question of who you want to be ultimately reflects your attitude and beliefs about life itself.

The decision of who you want to be will make a far bigger impact on your dream, your success, and your happiness than anything else. From my interaction with all the great people I have met throughout my professional life, I realized that what makes them happy is not so much their success or their possessions; rather, it is who they are as individuals, the difference they make around them, the way they help other people in their personal change process, and the joy they see in the eyes of those they impact. Success comes to successful people. It may sound like a cliché, but it makes a lot more sense than some of the ignorant assumptions that success comes from resources, education, or support. Who you are, manifests your world more than any material possession.

To decide how great you want to be, requires as a prerequisite that you're clear on what you pursue, and what it will require to get there. This will require uncompromising commitment and resilience from you.

When I was a teenager, I always struggled with defining what I wanted to become in life, contrary to my brother, two years younger than me. During one of those "mother and children" interactions, Mom asked us what we wanted to do as a profession in the future. At that very moment, I suddenly went blank in my head; whereas my brother, without hesitation, proclaimed that he wanted to become an aeronautics engineer. I wondered, in my 17-year-old teen's head: "Where did he get that from? What on earth is aeronautics engineering anyway?!" I knew it had something to do with airplanes and things, but I didn't know any more than that; but my 15-year-old brother was very clear on what he wanted, and he even edified us with some detailed information on the profession. Wow!! From that day on, as I recall, this purpose informed all of my brother's life decisions: what he studied in school, where he wanted to travel for his studies, who he connected with later in his life, and even how his vacation time was geared toward his dream. After seven long years of postgraduate studies, he graduated with an MSc in Aeronautical Engineering.

Today, looking back on that episode of my life, I understand that it does not matter the age or the season you decide to give a new direction to your existence; the key is for you to own your future, never allowing yourself to be under any kind of external pressure. You are the one to decide who you become in life, at a time right for you. Nobody should decide or influence your decision. You have to take full ownership of your future. You don't have to listen to friends and family or anybody else tell you who you are and who you are going to be. My own life is filled with examples to demonstrate that the life I have today is of my own making and is based on the choices I made, right or wrong.

Clear Visualization

I invite you to visualize, on a daily basis, who you want to be. Make this visualization vivid and precise. What professional style do you want to adopt? What kind of mother, father, husband, student, etc. do you want to be? What will be your dress style? How do you see yourself solving problems as a leader or coach? How good do you feel in your skin, knowing that people who feel good about themselves produce good results? Ask yourself these questions as you project yourself into the new you. Are you congruent with who you want to be, day in and day out? Are you taking the required actions to carry you along your journey?

I have spoken on stage, and I have led and am still leading people to become the best version of themselves through coaching. I am a best-selling author, and the question people ask me is: "How do you manage to be so enthusiastic and passionate about everything you do?" What I want you to know is that nothing happens by accident. You have to be intentional in what you want to achieve, and make a conscious effort to pursue your dream every day; visualize the person you want to be, and align all aspects of your life to that image. Who you become is the result of a conscious *decision*. Pay attention to the little things you need to do to reach your objective. Often, these little things will give you clues for uprooting and changing behaviors and thought processes that are incongruent with your ideal self. If you see yourself as being someone who puts great value on their health, and you eat a lot of junk food, you are putting distance between who you are and who you want to be. Take control of that habit, and change it and align it with who you want to be.

Have a Vision Board

Some people wrongly believe that vision boards are bogus. I can tell you that they work. Try it; set it up, and you will see the difference in your change management process. A vision board creates a sacred space that displays what you want to achieve, and brings it to life. It's not simply about placing an image on a board and manifesting what you want. When you create a vision board, and you place it in a space where you will see it often, you essentially end up doing short visualization exercises throughout the day. Visualization is one of the most powerful mind exercises you can express. You may have noticed the preparation that athletes go through before a competition; they create a clear picture of the competition ahead, and they imagine every step of the event.

Your vision board should focus on how you want to feel, not just on things that you want to get. Don't get me wrong; material things are important. However, the more you focus on how you want to feel, the more it will come to life. For example, on my vision board, I have an elastic training band. Every time I see it, it makes me feel like stretching myself, and never settling for less. I also have something representing whale song; when I see this on my board, it brings back that particular sound that whales make, and it reminds me to always seek strength deep inside myself.

One key rule about vision boards is that there aren't any rules. Your vision board is a reflection of your own inspiration and greatness aspiration. You can make it what you want.

Being Is Not About Setting Goals

Who you want to be isn't a goal. You are whoever you decide to be. Goals are set because external expectations take time to materialize. Deciding who you are committed to being in your life does not. The moment you decide that you are going to be a happy, enthusiastic, passionate person, you become one. Simply make sure that all of your actions are geared toward that new persona you have chosen to be: courageous, strong, committed, resilient, and unshakable.

On the example I gave you earlier about my brother, don't get me wrong. My brother is a freak. This basically never happens. In my case, I had no clue what I wanted to be. It is fair to say that most of us have no clue what we want to do with our lives—even after we finish school, even after we get a job, and even after we're making money. In my case, between the ages of 20 and 24, I changed career aspirations so many times that I don't have enough fingers to count. And even after I had a business up and running, it took another two years to clearly define what I wanted to achieve. Today, all is in place.

The idea of deciding who you want to be might sound scary to some people—it was scary for me for many years. If you are feeling the way I did then, you need to reconcile yourself with the source of your fear; you have to ditch the false idea that deciding what you want to be implies changing your surroundings. What you should understand is that no change can take place until you decide to initiate that change, and until you decide to change yourself. Remember that nothing is forced upon you; you have the choice to be either an active actor in your life, or to be just a passive individual at the mercy of every storm in your life, and accept that you will have to navigate in the sea of sameness.

As you apply the Greatness Trilogy concepts, I invite you to start visualizing your ideal self, to see opportunities opening up to you. I want you to conceptualize the "you" that is extroverted, confident, and courageous. As the leader you will become, I encourage you to see yourself as someone who is empathetic, thoughtful, courageous, and positive; someone who has the maturity to be in control and to take action, and someone who has the sense of humor to see the world as a place filled with incredible fun, enjoyment, and adventure, not just sacrifice and drudgery. I want you to see the new you, doing your best to contribute, and trying to pursue options to help others while simultaneously helping yourself; and finally, to see yourself as someone who is devoted to continuous growth, and teaching others to do the same.

That visualization must be specific, clear, and compelling to you. You are that person, free from fears related to internal and external influences. Believe that you have full control of your decision as to who you are, what you want to do, and ultimately, how great you want to be, based on the actions you take.

On the flip side, when you don't have a clear vision of who you want to be, you are likely to become like the masses, shaped and molded by your genetics, environment, or both. You become your default behaviors, and life becomes a game of luck and circumstance. As a result, you find yourself trapped in a position dictated to you by fate or chance.

Protect the new YOU.

You now know exactly who you want to be. The time has come to protect the new you, and to showcase your culture add in all you do, in terms of your ability to adapt to the environment you're in and the people you interact with, but most importantly for you to bring value to the table.

You now have a clear and compelling vision of who you want to be. However, you must resist against the strains of your environment. If your built-in optimism and enthusiasm are in any way threatened by people in your surroundings, who are depressing and convey negativity, staying around them might influence or even lead you to doubt your new self. Be bold enough to separate yourself from naysayers of any kind. Simply be aware that to sustain your new persona, it will involve a lot of external challenges.

Decide How Great You Want to Be

To decide how great you want to be is not limited to improving yourself. You need to also consider the tangibles of your environment. What does your house look like? How is your appearance and the clothes you wear? If they don't reinforce the identity you want, change them. If you want to be a person who is healthy and fit, don't fill the refrigerator with junk food; instead, eat healthy and make physical exercise an integral part of who you are. Staying fit does not have to mean going to the gym. People who have become gym addicts have developed the habit gradually. Having a gym membership is not cheap; if on top of that, you can't sustain a weekly three to four times regimen, you'll be wasting your hard-earned cash. My advice to my students is to use their surroundings as their training ground. For those who find it challenging to maintain a regular visit to the gym, I have developed a program that will teach you how you can use your house effectively to keep and remain in top shape.

Once you've made changes to your environment, make changes to your relationships. If your friends don't reinforce the person you want to be, get some new friends. Loyalty to someone who is going to keep you living below what you truly desire, is false. At the very least, shift your time to spend more of it with people that you feel would more accurately represent your image. Make sure that your efforts to decide who you want to be aren't in conflict with your environment.

Don't allow those incongruences to take hold of your space. Start shaping your environment to be the mirror image of who you are.

I want you to have a crystal clear picture about who you want to be. Make your visualization compelling, meaningful, and specific. Most of all, make your image so inspiring that you will strive toward it every day. Ask yourself who you want to be, because you will become whatever your answer is to this question.

What you are building is your personal brand; in other words, what you are known for. Therefore, never allow anything, not even yourself, to undermine or stain your name. You must do everything in your power to protect it, do what it takes to make it grow, and preserve its value proposition.

Chapter 3

Take Action

You are all set. Now is the time to turn knowledge into results. Whatever you have identified as your dream or your passion, now has to materialize, and that materialization boils down to taking action.

Action taking is what will make real the new you that you want to become. No strategy and no plan of action will take you where you want to be, unless you stand up, roll up your sleeves, and work on it. If you truly want to achieve greatness, you have to refuse to stand still. You have to refuse to navigate in the sea of sameness. The people who succeed are the ones who take action.

Your life will never ever change or improve if you do not take action. You may be equipped with tons of theory, you may have attended motivational self-development conferences from the best gurus out there, and you may have a good attitude and mindset for success, but if you just sit there dreaming your dream, nothing is going to come out of it. Action is the basis of all success. Every action may not give success, but at the same time, no success is possible without action.

Your life is only the result of the choices you make daily. Those choices elevate you or keep you rooted in your comfort zone. As a transformed individual who understands and who has decided to apply the Greatness Trilogy concept—Leadership, Fitness, and Spirituality—you know where you are going to, and you are ready to do what it takes to make your dream come true; not for selfish reasons, but rather to answer the call for an urgent situation you have identify, in your family, in your community, and in the world. The actions you will take are not triggered by your egocentric considerations. Intentionally, you have decided your intent by answering the call for a cause greater than your little self. You know that by adopting an altruist attitude toward the accomplishment of your mission, this will make you the true action-orientated individual you are.

You know what you need to do, and you are an action taker. You don't just voice an intention, because you know that talk is cheap. You have seen too many people around you who talk about all the wonderful things that they would like to do in respect to their dreams, but they never seem to get past the talking stage. The passion driving you is so strong that you know that action is priceless. Nothing happens without action. It's the fuel that takes you from where you are to where you want to be.

The Early Bird Catches the Worm

This is the moment to act. Overthinking about the task at hand will take you nowhere; it will keep you at ground zero. Too much thinking kills the momentum. Most people overanalyze because they are overwhelmed with sudden fear. This is normal. Your cognitive system senses that you are about to step out of your comfort zone; to protect you, it raises the alarm to prevent you from getting hurt. It's a survival instinct mechanism. Don't be deterred by it.

You are about to achieve something that will change your life and, potentially, the lives of many people around you. It's time to stand your ground against the old you, and to move confidently toward your goal. Overanalyzing will stop you in your stride, and you will give up. Instead, move forward and get your cognitive system to readjust to the new territory you want to explore and conquer. You are no longer like the masses who are tetanized by fear and picture the worst possible outcome for themselves. Those people have a negativity bias; their minds have become tainted by illusions of not succeeding. The key for you is to quiet the noise within, and just get into action immediately.

Along the way, you will experience failures. A transformational process is never a smooth ride. However, what you need to understand is that the failures and setbacks you encounter are only feedback on the actions you need to revisit and improve. Disconnect "failure" from "being unable," because failure is an important element in your process. You may have failed, but as long as you improve upon your previous attempts, you are okay; and success will meet with you at the end of your journey.

Finally, take action, and stop thinking too much. Pull up your sleeves and get on with it. If you remain resilient, you will get to know yourself truly, and be amazed and overjoyed with your final achievement. Just do it—Nike's slogan is so true. Take action, and you will be surprised at what you can achieve. The time to do it is N.O.W.: **N**o **O**pportunity **W**asted.

You have been presented with a golden opportunity to make your dream come true; grab it, and don't allow life to pass you by, making you wonder what could have been. The best way to know is to take action right away. As you do that, your **F.E.A.R.**—**F**alse **E**vidence **A**ppearing **R**eal—will disappear, your sight will be sharpened, your mind strengthened, and the way will be cleared to your greater life, because time waits for

Take Action

no one. Be the person you see, and be the person that you know, deep down inside of yourself, you can be—not tomorrow, not next week, month, or year, but today—be an action taker and a change maker.

"The only man who never makes mistakes is the man who never does anything."
– Theodore Roosevelt

Chapter 4

Become a Greatness Fanatic

*"Leadership and greatness come
to those who follow through.
Who stand for near-flawless execution."*
– Robin S. Sharma

Quick recap:

- You have selected your dream to fulfill.
- You have decided how great you want to be.
- You have set a plan of action, bearing in mind the three key elements of the Greatness Trilogy: Leadership, Fitness, and Spirituality.

You will now decide to be a "greatness fanatic."

The dictionary defines a fanatic as "a person filled with excessive and single-minded zeal, especially for an extreme cause." Your extreme cause has taken you out of your comfort zone, to resiliently pursue your dream and never look back.

If I ask you where you are at this point of your journey to greatness, after making the Greatness Trilogy concepts an integral part of who you are and how you operate, I have no doubt that the answer will be clear in your head. I believe that you wouldn't need to think twice about what to reply.

When you look back at where you were, what do you see? What is it about the new you that appeals to you? You have gathered all you need in order to build something far greater than yourself, and now is the time for you to keep believing and be a greatness fanatic.

What Does It Take to Become a Greatness Fanatic?

Let's be clear: Achieving greatness is not instantaneous; it has to be earned. If you want to succeed, you have to recognize that in the first place, as an individual, you are not already great, and that you are only aspiring to greatness. Through sweat and continuous efforts, you will condition yourself to be committed and resilient. Many people in life realistically do not want to put in the effort over a sustained period of time to actually achieve their objective. They are looking for "short-cuts" to success, which in many ways do not exist, forgetting that only hard work brings success. Moreover, becoming a "greatness fanatic" is about being dependable and disciplined, and ultimately being able to condition yourself to make that notion a part of you. For example, a professional athlete who is preparing for the Olympics will follow a routine prior to competition (practice, workouts, analyzing the competition or course), so that they can be in their best physical and mental state to compete. The focus they develop in the process, and the goal they want to reach, leads them to becoming a fanatic of what they are working toward, which is to win the number one spot on the podium.

A greatness fanatic is that individual who is committed to success, whose inputs are consistent over time, and who knows that the price of greatness is based on taking small actions a great number of times.

Becoming a greatness fanatic implies acting with intention. In other words, knowing what is required and doing what it takes to get there. There is no doubt that actions and results will not always reflect intentions, but as one moves toward "greatness," they should have a better idea of what "inputs" actually deliver "outputs." Mistakes will be made on the way—that is human nature—but there will be a better grasp on what is more likely to work out.

Becoming a greatness fanatic requires the strict application of a process that includes three key elements:

1. A compelling vision
2. A strong reason to follow through
3. A daily review of the vision, to feel it and make it an integral part of your focus.

There is a part in the brain called the reticular activating system (RAS). It is the part of the brain that determines what you notice around you. The RAS is very important because, when goals are set and you are very clear on the motivation, and you also have strong enough reasons, which you review regularly, they become a part of you, and you will be sensitized to see things that will help you get to your objective. The RAS registers what is important for you and puts it in the forefront of your life. In order to see lasting change, you will need to raise your standards. When you are serious about your transformation process, whatever you do toward your vision, endeavor to change it from "I SHOULD" to "I MUST." In order to get to that point, you need to RAISE YOUR STANDARDS.

Being a greatness fanatic requires that you raise your standards by backing them up with rituals. Rituals are where the driving force is. In other words, you visualize what you want to achieve, and you break it

Become a Greatness Fanatic

down into small actions that you will take on a daily basis. That way, you will get the momentum, and you will not get overwhelmed. The power to do those things will come from the inside and will become rituals.

Your rituals define you. For example, a gym fanatic wakes up in the morning; his gym equipment is ready, and he is ready to go and exercise. No matter how he feels, he will do whatever that ritual is.

Successful people do rituals that contribute to their success by applying an accumulation of little step-by-step actions toward their compelling vision, and feeling it and making it real before they even see it.

You will pursue your vision adamantly because you know that it is something the world needs, not just you. Being a greatness fanatic means that you care about other people.

You become a greatness fanatic when you enjoy giving your best all the time, in everything you do, and making it your standard. You actually condition your brain to believe and to perform according to the new character you embody, despite the inevitable challenges. You are so focused on your vision that you become accountable to the community or group of people that you want to serve. You condition yourself to always give the very best of yourself no matter what.

I am sure that along your journey to this point, you have encountered your fair share of successes and failures. As you have acquired more of both under your name, you have learned from each experience, and you now have the meaning of what it takes to be great and why.

You have realized that it was not the sporadic thrills that were the greatest learning experiences for you, but rather the long winding road with potential unexpected challenges around each corner. Each challenge that you overcame along the way compounded into major gains, which led you to appreciate what *greatness* truly means. I have no doubt that you have come to learn that the journey to greatness is not about overnight successes or flashes of excellence, but about the periods of consistent repeatable habits toward your vision.

Now you got it. Deep down, you know the investment you needed to get this far, in terms of energy, time, and maybe financial. There is no denying that inside, you have the drive to do even better, motivated as you are by your achievement to date. You know that to remain on that momentum, one year, five years, or ten years or more from now, is having, on a regular basis, experiences that make you feel that your life is making continuous progress—because PROGRESS = HAPPINESS. When you can make progress on a regular basis, you feel alive, you are encouraged to do what your soul desires, you can expand, you can grow, and you can change; but better than change, you can progress.

I encourage people who want to embark on a transformational journey, to apply the old adage: "If you want to take the island, burn the boat." When the boats are burnt, there is no turning back; there is no choice but to find a way to make things work. Despite the stern challenges, the driving force becomes **H.O.P.E.**: **H**old **O**n, **P**ain **E**nds.

5 Reasons Why You Must Be a Greatness Fanatic:

1. **You believe in yourself** – Step one of your journey was to bring you to select a dream, to identify something you are passionate about. The idea is for you to believe in yourself. If you don't believe in yourself, then no one else will. Don't look to others to define your confidence; you get to do that for yourself, and you did to this point.

2. **You know that nothing is for free** – You made the required sacrifice to reach the point you are currently at, because you took action accordingly.

You paid the price; despite the obstacles, you never gave up. You knew that the world wasn't going to deliver your dreams on a platter. Your passion is yours, and you know that only you can bring it to fruition: the book you want to write, the business you want to start, the coaching course you want to take, the change of career you envision, the new physical shape you want to be in. You've learned along this journey that if you sit around waiting for your passion to materialize, it is not going to happen. You have to go out and *get it*. You have to do the work, and you did it. Well done, champion!

3. **You are your best cheer leader** – You may have criticized your failures in the past, blasting your mistakes, and licking your wounds from bad decisions. But now you know that those failures and challenges are the bridges that took you to the other side. Today, you can stand proud for the things you have accomplished. Acknowledge your victories and be proud of them. This motivates you to even higher levels of performance. No mountain will be too high for you; no failure will be a showstopper for you.

4. **You don't keep your accomplishments quiet** – This is an important milestone. You are now the person you always wanted to be. You are making a difference in your community, and people love the

value you bring into their lives. You refused to work silently because you know that there is no such thing as silent success. Rather, it produces the absence of visibility. You have been rewarded for your hard work because you knew that the caveat to that statement is that *others must be aware of your accomplishments.* You took the steps to make your accomplishments known. This is not bragging; it's *showcasing.*

5. **Ultimately, you are the maestro** – You now understand that ultimately, your life is about you. Is this a selfish thought? Absolutely not. It's not even an arrogant one. You came to the realization that in this world, you are only competing against … yourself. You determined how great you wanted to be, and now the results are there to speak on your behalf; and you are now a greatness fanatic, because you know the true meaning of being the best version of yourself and what it took you to get there.

This is what greatness feels and tastes like. With the confidence you've gained, the sky is now your limit; only you can decide how far you can go. Yes, keep your options infinite. Make your life a journey of infinite possibilities. I'm proposing that your real game be to always strive to keep your options opened as long as you can, and I mean as long as you have the privilege to be on this planet. There is no turning back. Always crave to add a "dot-dot-dot" to all your endeavors. What I mean is that you never see a closed door when the going gets tough. Similarly, you don't become complaisant when things are going well. For every mountain you climb, you know that there is another one ahead and that you are equipped for the challenge. If you meet failure on the way, that's okay. There is no need for self-judgement; just add a "yet" at the end of a self-judgment. For example: I don't have the right skills for the situation … yet; I can't see the way out … yet. Adding a "yet" to sentences about yourself is empowering. Keep that mindset, and you will become unstoppable; and as a bonus … You'll become the full time greatness fanatic you worked so hard for.

Chapter 5

Seek Spiritual Fulfillment

We've reached the fifth stage of your transformational journey. Let me warn you, this is a touchy topic. When I shared this title with some friends, the first question they asked me was: "What does spirituality have to do with leadership and fitness?" Most people cannot fathom the different between religion and spirituality. Before we move on, let's remove any concern that you may have on the meaning of those two words. Let's establish the difference between religion and spirituality.

According to the dictionary, **religion** is a specific set of organized beliefs and practices, usually shared by a community or group.

Spirituality, on the other hand, is more of an individual practice, and has to do with having a sense of peace and purpose. It is the quality of being concerned with the human spirit or soul, as opposed to material or physical things.

Some people see no connection between leadership, fitness, and spirituality. For them, being successful is a matter of working hard and never giving up. Some describe themselves as *self-made*; in other words, they owe their success to their sole effort. Some arguments could be formulated against such views. There is nothing fundamentally wrong with those views; however, in my opinion, there is more to (lasting) success and greatness than hard work, dedication, and knowledge.

Some people with whom I have shared the Trilogy, see the inseparable connection between spirituality and the other two elements of the Trilogy: leadership and fitness. Spirituality is being seen as the force that keeps one rooted and serene in all situations, good or challenging. Through the spiritual element, one measures the power and grace of an entity higher and bigger than oneself; an entity without which one wouldn't know how to be detached from their little and finite self.

Being spiritually fulfilled is the ongoing alignment of self with a higher entity, knowing that **"the Universe doesn't give you what you ask for with your thoughts; it gives you what you demand with your actions."** – Steve Maraboli.

Some people ascribe greatness onto the Universe or God, as being the source of everything. Whether that entity is God, Allah, Buddha, etc., one thing that reconciles most people is that the Source is the same for all, and that the name they respectively refer to as the Source, is the personification of God, brought down to their level of understanding of who He is. This group of people believe that God, being the source of everything, should have all glory given to Him, and they ascribe greatness onto Him.

Whatever you subscribe to in terms of your spiritual beliefs, your destiny will find its source in your spiritual fulfillment. It is your heritage. It's the course of your life that is more than a potential. It is made up of your values, of what drives you in life.

In today's fast-paced culture (certainly in the West), there is a growing hunger for ways in which we can nourish our souls, and tune in more to our "being," rather than our "doing" selves, to create more meaning, purpose, and fulfillment in our lives.

As an antidote to the high-tech world, increasing numbers of individuals are beginning to ask existential questions to understand who they really are, and to discover their real purpose in life. Some are turning to mindfulness, meditation, and other approaches, such as yoga, to explore ways in which they can calm their minds, increase their well-being, and feel more connected to themselves, life, and others.

All these questions about life, are bringing more and more people to show interest in "spirituality," and to get to the awareness that we are more than material minds and bodies; we are complex beings made up of a material and a spiritual body. There is more and more of a need to create a balance between those temporally inseparable entities, by taking care of them in order to achieve balance, wholeness, well-being, and harmony, physically and spiritually.

The concept of spirituality will vary from one person to another. For some people, exploring their spirituality may mean turning to a higher power for guidance, or they may have a defined faith; but for others, the traditional, defined ways don't suit them or bring the fulfillment that they are looking for. So, if this is you, you'll need to find other ways to establish this for yourself. What do you believe in? What is that force within that keeps you going no matter what? Where do you get your source of inspiration from? Answering those questions is fundamental, as it may involve a search within. Or you may explore and blend different approaches to find a way of connecting to and exploring your inner world, and finding a "spiritual practice" that works for and feels most meaningful, nurturing, and supportive for you.

There is not a cut and paste formula to discovering one's source of spiritual fulfillment. All that matters is that you know what brings you alive, what fills you up spiritually, and what gives you a distinctive sense of belonging to something greater than yourself. Nature and nurture are closely related, so it may involve finding ways to nourish yourself by finding out what brings you alive and fulfills you. This may involve connecting with a sense of a greater presence, which could be the greater field of intelligence (universal "mind" or universal life force), or your higher self, God, spirit, nature—whatever term resonates and feels in alignment for you. It's that pure consciousness, energy, and intelligence that creates life and animates matter at an atomic level, from wave to particle, and turns pure energy and atoms into "form."

You may find yourself seeking time for solitude and reflection, or wanting to spend more time in nature, or cultivating practices and rituals that help you feel more centred and grounded in your life. All of this doesn't mean that you have to achieve some elusive state of "Nirvana"; enlightenment doesn't have to be found doing endless hours of yoga, meditating in a monastery, or sitting on top of a mountain (as great as those experiences can be). Cultivating spirituality and inner aliveness can happen in the small things you do each and every day. You can start right here, right now, by becoming more mindful and paying attention to what's most meaningful and important to you in your life—you can practice "everyday enlightenment."

Sometimes people shy away from the word "spirituality," and assume it's tied into a defined religion or specific dogma or doctrine. However, our "spirit" can simply be defined as "the force within a person that is believed to give the body life, energy, and power," and "the inner quality or nature of a person."

It's our quality of "aliveness" and the way that we cultivate consciousness, awareness, and understanding of what is within us and in the world around us, that makes us start asking powerful questions such as "Who" am I? Who is the "I" that is able to experience and observe life? By bringing awareness to this, we can observe that we are not our thoughts, but we are the ones that are able to observe and think those thoughts—the consciousness behind the thoughts. And this consciousness is part of the bigger, unified field of consciousness that all beings are connected to. So we realise that we are all connected to one another. If we start to experience life at this level, we can cultivate greater peace and joy in our lives, as we become less attached to externals and the outer circumstances of our lives, and become more focused on our inner experiences.

However, your spiritual fulfillment is not something that you will be able to complete in your lifetime. It's something that's ongoing and works on the eternal level. It's about you making the choices about how you want your life to go, according to what you believe in, allowing yourself to claim spiritual fulfillment, and to live according to what that is for you.

Spiritual fulfillment means the realization of your true self—of who you are. You can't realize that just through your mind or anything that this world can bring to you. That realization is an inner experience in which you know that you are not only just enough, but you are always more than enough. That means there's nothing that exists or is in your life that can ever stop you from your spiritual fulfillment.

Spiritual fulfillment is a knowing that who you are overcomes all things that could ever challenge you. It's an understanding that you are complete. It's not something that we can fully speak to in this world. We can't show it to you or hold it up to you and say, "Here is your spiritual fulfillment." It's something you already know inside of yourself, or you know enough about it that you want it. This is known as *soul transcendence*, which is the very highest and most inclusive or holistic level of human consciousness, behaving, and relating, as ends rather than means, to oneself, to significant others, to human beings in general, to other species, to nature, and to the Universe.

So, if you want spiritual fulfillment, if you want soul transcendence, then it is yours to have. You can have what you want. It's just a matter of you choosing what is already yours and prepared for you. That preparation is spiritual. In some ways, what that means is that, as the leader, as the coach, as the influencer you are, you have a mission clearly defined; you release yourself from your lower nature, i.e. that self-centered persona whose focus is predominantly on earthy material existence. You let that go so that it no longer has the importance or the attachment that it once had. Instead, you open yourself to having a heart of service, where you allow yourself to take the back seat, and give the front, raw, to your tribe.

*"This is the gift of gratitude: in order to feel it,
your ego has to take a back seat.
What shows up in its place is
greater compassion and understanding.
Instead of being frustrated, you choose
appreciation. And the more grateful you become,
the more you have to be grateful for."
– Oprah Winfrey*

Seek Spiritual Fulfillment

Your spiritual fulfillment is the force that sustains you. Even though you can't see it, it's built in you and it is there for you. All you have to do is have faith and tap into it for guidance. It is about connecting with your soul and knowing what your purpose in life is—what you are here to do until you transit from earth school. Some call it **"your big why."** This is what you are wanting to attain here, or your destiny, in this lifetime. Another way to think of this is that it is your contract that you signed up for before you came to earth school.

Once you are spiritually fulfilled, it means that nothing can stop you. There are no obstacles that can detour you on your path because your soul knows that anything can be attained with the power of thought. You are complete and fulfilled as you venture forth. Spiritual fulfillment is also knowing that you are not alone on your journey. Your God, the power in you, is on your side, so who can be against you? He is here to team up with you and cheer you along the way. When you are spiritually fulfilled, you recognize that you are in earth school to learn lessons and experience things; you start to remember that your mission to the world is greater than anything you could ever have imagined. You have a purpose-driven life. You know where you have been, you know where you are, and you know where you are going. The Spirit of God is well established in you. It illuminates your understanding and profound appreciation for the way it works in you, and you start exercising into the truth of your being. It is a valuable and joyful exercise of patience, kindness, and happiness.

Spiritual fulfillment is your destiny. It is your heritage. It's the course of your life that is more than a potential. It is a given. Spiritual fulfillment will take you places. You no longer perceive life from the physical universe. You know that there's something bigger and higher than that finite realm. However, let's be clear; you may not experience the completion of your spiritual fulfillment in your lifetime. It's something that works on an eternal level. It's about you making the choice, allowing yourself to claim spiritual fulfillment, and to live according to your understanding of what that is for you.

Spiritual fulfillment is your true identity in direct connection with the spiritual Universe, the source of all knowledge. In order for you to have a clear understanding of what the Universe has for you, you can't realize that just through your mind or anything that this world can bring to you. That realization is an inner experience in which you know that you are not only just enough, but you are always more than enough.

Seek Spiritual Fulfillment

That means there's nothing that exists or is in your life that can ever stop you from your spiritual fulfillment. it will help you overcome all things that could ever challenge you. Your understanding of life is sharpened and you know that you never walk alone. You are filled with a certain level of rested assurance about everything you do. Thus, the understanding of being complete. You can't explain it with mere words, but you know deep down that you have it. This is how you transcend to a higher level of awareness. You start seeing the world in a different way and you start seeing others from a spiritual perspective.

According to Maslow, it refers to "the very highest and most inclusive or holistic levels of human consciousness, behaving, and relating, as ends rather than means, to oneself, to significant others, to human beings in general, to other species, to nature, and to the cosmos." However, self-actualization is the first step before transcendence. Before transcending yourself, however, you need to be self-actualized.

The foundation of self-transcended people is caring for others and higher ideals.

Chapter 6

Live a Life of Service

"The end of all knowledge should be service to others."
– Cesar Chavez

Wouldn't it be helpful if we could all start our lives with these two questions: **What is the meaning of life? What am I here for?**

1. *What is the meaning of life?*

The question pertains to the significance of living. Depending on your cultural background and belief, different components will make up your answer to this question. We live in societies where wondering too insistently on the question may see you being categorized as being weird or "off your rocker." However, the question is valid.

What if the question was asked differently? "What is the meaning of (my) life?" Adding "my" to the question forces you to personalize the concern. This question should be asked in a more specific manner by adding the word "my" to "What is the meaning of (my) life?" It simplifies the problem, but it doesn't solve it. At most, putting the focus on ourselves gives us a *chance* to answer the question. In order to find our purpose in life, we need to dig below the surface and ask ourselves even more specific questions. We need to understand our values, talents, and potentials. We need to ask ourselves 3 questions.

For all schools of belief, once you are spiritually fulfilled, you cannot answer that question from an intellectual perspective, because the best you will be able to do is to answer from a materialistic point of view, in terms of being successful in your job or in your business, having possessions, having a beautiful and healthy family, etc. All possible answers are selfishly driven. All that we have in our lives is finite, and we are never satisfied with what we have. The novelty of things seems to die out so quickly. We are always in search of something new, something to satisfy our insatiable egos. Many self-development books have attempted to find an answer by teaching their readers to focus on themselves to find the true meaning of life. They never seek to offer an answer by advising ways to self-discovery from the spirit within, the highest entity within us. The Bible says, in Genesis 2:7, that "… the LORD God formed a man from the dust of the ground and breathed into his nostrils the breath of life, and the man became a living being." Man only became a living being when God breathed His spirit in him. Therefore, the meaning of life can only be understood from the perspective of the creator. You cannot find the meaning of life by looking into yourself. You did not create yourself; therefore, you cannot tell what you were created for. Let's clarify this point. If someone handed you a machine that you had never seen before, you wouldn't know what it is used for; the invention itself wouldn't know what it was created for. Only the creator of the machine would be able to edify people on what his machine is used for. Similarly, for us humans to understand the meaning of life, we need to tap into the spirit of God in us, the source of all knowledge. We cannot access that level of understanding unless we operate at the spirit level. God is spirit, and he can only have a conversation with us in the spirit realm.

2. *What am I here for?*

To answer that existential question, one has to be clear on what their purpose is. Once you know your purpose, your higher-level mission, you are in a better disposition to identify what services will be required to be of service to others. The purpose of your life goes beyond any personal fulfillment—your academic achievements, your marriage to your spouse, or even your happiness. Your purpose stands far taller than anything you could accomplish on this earth school.

"What am I here for?" is, without a shadow of a doubt, a difficult question to answer. This is the case because we live in a world based on an individualist perspective. We use "I" because we are driven by self-centeredness; we tend to start from our own perspective. We have a continuous battle against self-promotion rather than elevating others.

The most classic symptom of this issue is the predominant use of "I" rather than "we." We routinely say: "I" want this, "I" want that, "I" did this, or "I" did that, rather than "we" want this or that, or "we" did this or that. Since time immemorial, this has been a recurring situation. For those familiar with the Bible, a dispute arose among Jesus's disciples, as to which one of them was the greatest. Jesus answered: "Let the greatest among you become as the youngest, and the leader as one who serves." Even in those days, focus was on "self." Very few human beings would be ready to dedicate their lives to serving others. We have been raised in competitive environments, where survival of the fittest is the rule of the game. Everybody wants to mark their territory, and they will fight fiercely to protect it. You see that in families, between brothers and sisters, in schools, and in corporate environments, where self-centeredness can turn nasty, for the sake of promotion scavenging. Humans become like crabs in a bucket, each trying to get out first but always being pulled down by other crabs trying to do the same.

Being of service to others is only possible if you begin from the right place: the spirit of God within you—the power higher than you, opening you to having a heart of service, focusing more on the needs around you than on your own. The fascinating thing is that each of us has a different life purpose. For example, your purpose might be to become a coach and author. Someone else's might be to become a small business owner, or to be a farmer. The options are endless for what a person's life purpose might be. But there is one common thread that runs through every human being's life purpose: We all are here to serve the world and, in some way, improve it. That may sound like a daunting task, but it isn't.

When your purpose is predominantly to chase material things, you quickly realize that there is more joy in pursuing less, than can be found in pursuing more. In many ways, this is a message that we already know to be true. We know that possessions don't equal joy. And we know that our life's purpose is far much greater than spending our time chasing them.

When we see what has been happening in the world in recent months with the Covid-19 pandemic, and the devastating impact it has had on the entire world's activities, we can humble ourselves and measure how fragile life is. A virus ascendance that has rattled stock markets, disrupted the daily lives of millions, and resulted in the heartbreaking deaths of thousands of people around the globe, is a reminder that life is just a moment, and circumstances can change overnight unexpectedly. Being aware of this is so important that it brings you to realize that the time for you to make a difference is now. Why? Because tomorrow might never come. You have to build the mindset that your mission on this planet is to be of service to others. This means preparing yourself accordingly. The service that you render to your family, to your community, to your city, to your country, or to the world, will be the reflection of how you feel about yourself inside, and how you do everything you do. As you render service, you should not look for anything from anybody for simply doing your best. You don't expect a pat on the back.

Live a Life of Service

I imagine that you have your daily routine to prepare yourself for the day; for example, you get up early, you pray and meditate, you do your morning workout, you take a shower while listening to your favorite music, etc. So, you prepare yourself to be the best service provider there is. You want to bring your best out there. That pat on the back should only come when you have exceeded what most people consider exceptional work, or have gone above and beyond what is expected. Don't expect a pat on the back for a normal task you are supposed to be doing anyway as part of your regular daily activity. There is nothing exceptional about it.

Being of service is not about you. It's about your loved ones, your team, your community, your country, your contribution to changing the world for the better, and having pride in yourself after that. It's not about what others think or feel about you; it's about how you feel about yourself.

"The best way to find yourself is to lose yourself in the service of others."
– Mahatma Gandhi

This is how your leadership qualities will be manifested, and how you will impact people around you.

> *"Leadership is service, not position."*
> – Tim Fargo

Once you integrate what follows, your life will start being a purpose-driven life, and your existence will have a completely different meaning.

Your life is short. In case you had not realized it, and as we said earlier, life is short, and it can take a turn in an unexpected way— e.g., Covid-19. Therefore, the time for you to be a great service provider is now. You only get one shot at it. Time is an opportunity, and it goes by quick. And once you waste it, you can't get it back. So, make the most of it. When you over-focus on yourself, your possessions, and all tangible stuff, you quickly realize that they steal your time and energy. They drive you away from who you really are in relation to the world you live in. All tangibles require unending maintenance to be cleaned, maintained, fixed, replaced, and removed. They steal your precious focus, time, and energy, and you don't even notice it… until it's too late.

Live a Life of Service

Your life is unique. You are unique. "You were powerfully and wonderfully made," says the bible. Your look, your personality, your talents, and the people who have influenced your life, have made you special. That's right; you did not make yourself special. Your Creator surrounded you with what was required to make you who you are. Therefore, what can you do to be of service to the world around you? What do you need to do to be of service to the world today?

There are 7.8 billion people on this planet. Did you know that each and every one of them has a unique mission to accomplish? That includes you and me. Find your purpose, and get on with your unique mission.

Your life is meaningful. Far more than success, your heart desires significance because significance lasts forever. Your God-given significance will not be manifested through what you do for yourself, but rather through how you serve others.

Your life is meant to inspire. As long as you are in this earth school, you want to make footprints worth following. Nobody ever changed the world by following someone else. No, you get inspired by others; you learn from their experience and from the knowledge you acquire, and you build up your own path and personality to impact the world and inspire others to do the same. Anything less than that may briefly impress but never inspires. Remember the story of Les Brown that I shared with you when we started this journey? Mr. Brown realized that his mission would not be complete until he teaches and shares his knowledge with the new generation of motivational speakers. He believes that passing on the baton is fundamental if one wants to leave a legacy.

We've all been created to share our knowledge and to help others rise up and be the best they can be.

Your life is important and it is needed. Your heart and soul make you valuable to the world. Don't sacrifice your important role in this world by settling for possessions that can be purchased with money. The Bible says: "And what do you benefit if you gain the whole world but lose your own soul? Is anything worth more than your soul?" Is anything worth more than having a purpose-driven life focused on being of service to other people? Think for one second of all the people who spend their whole lives never knowing what their greater purpose is. They were beautifully created, but they never asked themselves this existential question: "What am I here for?" This is why it is rightly said that graveyards are filled with unfulfilled dreams; lives that maybe ended with regrets…

Your life deserves better. Joy, happiness, and fulfillment are found in the invisible things of life: love, hope, and peace. These are fruits of the spirit, and they cannot be purchased in shopping malls or anywhere else for that matter. Stop looking for them there. Having a life focused on material gains does not give contentment, because material possessions can never satisfy the deepest desires of the heart. Recently, I was having a conversation with my long-time friend of over 30 years. He is an amazing guy, inside and out—a successful businessman, a great family man, has a beautiful wife, and has done brilliant studies. He is the incarnation of success; yet he confided in me about the deep emptiness in his life, and the lack of peace and contentment he experiences daily.

This simply shows that a meaningful life is not defined by what you possess. It is about being real, being humble, and being able to share yourself and to touch the lives around you. Be reminded that your life is far too valuable to waste by chasing material possessions. Find more joy today by choosing to pursue "better" rather than "more." "Better" is found in the service you render to others.

Remember, there are 7.8 billion people in the world, and all 7.8 billion people are valuable and are needed to bring their contribution to the bettering of the world, each in their capacity.

> *"How will you serve the world?*
> *What do they need that your talent can provide?*
> *That's all you have to figure out."*
> – Jim Carrey

In order for you to serve the world effectively and with pleasure, you've got to be yourself. By being true to yourself, you can be true to others. I said earlier that we were all created unique and beautiful, worthy and powerful. This is why the world needs you. Your talents are unique, and no one else can be exactly like you. The uniqueness that you have is maybe something that only you can apply to make a difference in the life of one person out there. By embracing all that you are, by living life from a place of truth and high integrity, and by listening to your inner voice and intuition, not only will you feel great joy and fulfillment, but you will also learn how to be of service to those around you.

> *"The purpose of life is not to be happy.*
> *It is to be useful, to be honorable,*
> *to be compassionate, to have it make some*
> *difference that you have lived and lived well."*
> – Ralph Waldo Emerson

Live a Life of Service

Living a life of service is about embracing and sharing all that you are— your presence, your talents, your love, your know-how, etc.—with the rest of the world.

Below are some ways to live a life of service to the world. When you approach your life in this way, you'll find that it becomes much more meaningful.

1. **Treat your passion as an act of service to others**

    Most of us view our professional activities as ways to make money—fair enough. However, try putting a different spin on that perspective, and start seeing your activities as being a part of your service to the world. How does that feel?

    Whether you are a lawyer, a janitor, a coach, a mechanic, or a scientist, your job in some way impacts others. Therefore, how you do your job matters. When you do your job well, and you treat people around you with kindness and respect, you make your part of the world a much better place.

    Moreover, your job becomes more enjoyable when you view it as an act of service to the world. I remember the story of Maria, a charming middle-aged woman who used to clean our office space.

Every day, Monday to Friday, she was there doing her job with love and commitment. One day, her boss, who sometimes closed late, noticed that Maria sounded so happy and seemed to be enjoying her job. So, he asked her: "You seem so happy, Maria; what is happening in your life?" She had the most unexpected answer. With a big smile, she said: "I no longer push dust under the carpet." What she meant by that was that she was now doing her work with love, well aware that by doing so, she would be contributing by making life easier for those coming in the next morning, so that they may work in a clean environment. Maria was happy to see others happy because of the good service she was doing.

2. **Treat every task as important**

We tend to value tasks based on how much we can get paid for doing them. It is likely that no one pays you to clean your bathroom or to do your family's laundry. Therefore, we view those tasks as unimportant. But in fact, the opposite is true! Every task is important, especially when it involves making other people's lives better. The more directly you serve another human being, the more valuable that task is. For instance, in my mind, folding my daughter's clothes is just as important as the work that I do in the office. It's true that I don't

Live a Life of Service

get paid to fold her clothes, but that small act is valuable. When I take care of her clothing, I am showing her that I love her.

In the same way, you can have acts of service toward yourself. When I wake up in the morning, my first chore is to make my bed. Why do I make it a priority? Well! I feel that if I make my bed every morning, I have accomplished the first task of the day, and it gives me a small sense of pride and encouragement. Making my bed represents my first task of the day, and it prepares me for all the other tasks ahead. By the end of the day, that one task completed will have turned into many tasks completed.

So, remember that even the smallest task done in service to another, and to self, is important. Do even those small tasks well and with love.

3. Be on the alert for ways to serve

Most people have difficulty asking for help; typically, folks don't want to impose on anyone else. As a result, if you see someone struggling, don't just *offer* to help. That person likely won't take you up on it. *Just help.*

I remember, a couple of years ago, when I held a

mastermind in my house. It was an opportunity for me to inaugurate the space in my basement that I had just refurbished and transformed into a work area. I invited fifteen guests for the occasion. My friend offered, without me asking, to take me to a nearby place where I could hire a few chairs. She even brought in, later that day, a variety of tasty and well-presented finger foods. I never asked for it, but she offered to be of service to me. I offered to pay her but she refused. I felt a little uncomfortable with her kindness, but I understood and I accepted her act of kindness. At the end of the event, she decided to do even more by helping me clean up the place. WOW! Talk about being of service!

This just goes to show that taking the time to think about others, volunteering our time, and helping someone (like my friend did at my event or however else we might do it), has an immense impact on our overall happiness and fulfillment in our own lives. We all have this need inside of us to make a difference in someone else's life. In fact, so many people have a desire to make a difference.

We all have a desire to be seen, to be valued, and to be *truly heard.* In most cases when we spend time helping others, we not only feel good on the inside, but we feel valued by the person we are helping. I really felt valued by my friend, Carole. I felt like I mattered. We ALL have a desire to feel like we matter in this 7.8 billion people-packed world, and making a difference makes us feel like we matter. It makes us feel validated. It makes us feel like we are important.

No matter where we are in our lives, no matter what type of schedule we currently have, there is always a way to make a difference in somebody's life.

So, be on the alert. If you see someone with a need, try to fill it. Make serving others an activity that you naturally seek out throughout your day.

By the way, months down the stretch, that good friend of mine, Carole, became my wife. Maybe that was God's service to me, and an answer to my prayers, following a loss that wounded me so deeply two years earlier. I'm so blessed to have her in my life.

4. Serve without expectation of thanks

If you help others with an expectation of gratitude, or in order to receive something in return, you have missed the entire point. A life of service is a reward unto itself. When we serve others, it changes us for the better. First, it gives us a sense of confidence. If you can help others, you are a capable individual. You are no longer a child but an adult who can care for other people

Service also keeps us humble. In a world in which we often are being served, we easily can go down the misguided path of thinking that we are superior. It is important sometimes to be the person who serves, so that we keep our egos in check. It also helps us to make a connection with other people. When you serve another person, you are offering more than tangible assistance. You are offering love. And when that other person accepts, you've made a new connection.

So, don't serve with the expectation of a "thank you." Of course, it's nice when people express their gratitude, but serve others knowing that when you serve, you truly are the one who benefits. Consider adopting some of the above approaches to living your life in service to the world. When you do so, you will see your own life be transformed for the better.

"Service doesn't have to be big and grandiose to be meaningful and make a difference."
– Cheryl A. Esplin

Chapter 7

Get the Support You Need

We have seen throughout this book that the walk to greatness is not an easy one but a doable one. Like any endeavor in life, you will meet challenges along the way that might discourage you, and sometimes they might lead you to giving up. Preparedness is key in any process, and in order for you to successfully reach your objective, equip yourself with what will be required to stay the course.

Before getting the support you need, you've got to be aware of where you stand in terms of being able to identify what will help you move forward and be of service to others. Let's be clear; transformation is something that you embark on for yourself, as a starting point. You go through a transformational process because you want to be the best version of yourself before you can consider supporting others with their own challenges.

https://www.charlestchoreret.com/

Getting the support that you need encompasses anything that involves your transformation as a person. It means becoming the best you can be and reaching toward your potential. When you become a "better" person than you were yesterday (this does not mean better than another person), your life and its circumstances improve. This is usually achieved by looking internally and then changing the way you act externally. It's never an easy exercise to go through. By nature, we are not always ready to face our flaws. While it may be tempting to lead from the front on all matters concerning your personal development, humble yourself by recognizing that you are not all-knowing; in fact, nobody is. If you want to improve, you will have to be open on where the gaps in your knowledge and experience lie, and turn your attention to finding ways to close them. At this stage, writing a list is fundamental; it will guide you to be precise on what you need, so that you can have a better understanding of where your strengths and weaknesses are, and then build a strategy on how to pull resources you need in order to improve. I believe that being open and honest about where you stand, and finding ways to improve, can be a powerful strategy for building up the best version of yourself.

In all self-transformational processes, planning what you intend to do is essential. Writing down what you want is the first step. For example, ensure that you are choosing a coach who is right for you, based on what you want to achieve. It's important that you take time choosing a coach if you want a good return on your investment, and to reap the rewards of your coaching experience. There are many people who have derived huge benefits from, and extol the virtues of, their coach; whilst unfortunately, I know of others who have been disappointed and have felt that their experience just left them with a huge hole in their pocket. I can say something about it, because I was one of those people who did not do their due diligence before choosing a coach. Let me not go there, because I don't even want to remember how much money I lost. One thing is for sure: I learned from the experience, and I know better now.

How Do You Choose the Right Coach?

This is an important question, and it is the first one you should ask yourself. There are many ways to choose a coach, but fundamentally your search will be driven by these 6 questions:

1. What area of your life are you looking to make changes in?
2. Are you looking for help with being crystal clear on your vision?

3. Are looking for the best platform to pass on your message, through a book, speaking on stage, etc.?
4. What do you want to be different?
5. Are you at a crossroads and looking to gain clarity to help you move forward, or do you have a specific problem you would like to solve?
6. Are you looking for someone who will challenge your thinking, or someone who will build your confidence?

Taking some time to think about these questions before you start your search, will help you decide on the best resources you need in order to move forward and strive. If you have some ideas as to what you want to achieve, when you speak with prospective coaches, you should be able to gauge whether they can help you in the way you want.

Once you have gathered all the resources you need, you must remember that this process is about you. You may get yourself the right coach, but at the end of the day, only you will make it happen. You've got to put yourself in the right mental and spiritual dispositions as you go along your journey. You have to become a greatness fanatic, always bearing in mind that your success will depend upon the difference you will make in people that you will work with, and who will see you as an added value to their lives. Therefore, you will

Get the Support You Need

strive to become the best you can be by reaching toward your full potential. When you become a "better" person than you were yesterday (this does not mean better than another person), your life and its circumstances improve. This is usually achieved by looking internally and then changing the way you act externally. You will need to raise your standards. By that, I mean, like I said before, that you will adopt new habits and new rituals from what you were used to. As you raise your standards, you get closer to the vision of the new you. Remember, Rome was not built in one day.

Focus on progress, not on the change you want to achieve. Progress adds an aliveness to your journey. Don't work on change; change is automatic. Everything in life changes; it's inevitable. So, if you want to see real progress, focus on each step, and be the best you can be in completing them. You have to take control of the process, and start looking at your life in a completely different way.

Once you have identified the resources you need, it's time for you to put a strategy to move forward. I'm offering you 9 tips to consider on your road to greatness and enjoying a wildly successful life.

https://www.charlestchoreret.com/

1. Start Now

There's no time to be wasted. I was doing a Facebook live during the Covid-19 pandemic, and I asked the people present what they did during their time in confinement, in relation to their business, their personal lives, or their upcoming projects. I wanted to know the strategies they implemented to prepare themselves for the "new normal."

One of the participants wrote a comment and said that they didn't have any project, and that it was business as usual despite the prolonged confinement period.

First of all, it could not have been business as usual. Covid-19 brutally took the whole world out of its comfort zone. Therefore, preparing for the change ahead was only logical.

As the new person you have become, any time, no matter how challenging it is, is a good time to make progress and grow. Grab all opportunities to learn and to improve. Growth can only happen when you are clear on what you want for yourself, and when you take action accordingly.

Confinement during the pandemic was a great window of opportunity for me to work on my website and to add personal development content to my YouTube channel. This is just to emphasize that the time to start is NOW, because today is the right day to get the ball rolling. I encourage you to consider every day like a new beginning, because every day is a new opportunity to improve on whatever did not go as planned, and to try new things related not only to your business but also to your personal life.

Any season of your life is a good time to start: The time is **N.O.W.** (**N**o **O**pportunity **W**asted). Change will only take place when there is movement. Don't be a "pro-crastinator," but rather a pro-action taker.

> *"Tomorrow is promised to no one."*
> – Clint Eastwood

Your time for action is now.

2. Go One Step at a Time

Build a plan of action that includes steps. Remember that to eat an elephant, you should proceed one bite at a time. In other words, go about your transformational process step by step. There will be small goals and much bigger ones to attain. Go for those low hanging fruits, the smaller tasks, because they will encourage you to carry on; as for the bigger ones, break them, as much as possible, into smaller components. Don't focus so much on the change you want to achieve; rather focus on the progress you make, because progress is what will bring about the change you want, and will give you the motivation you need to press forward.

3. Learn from Those Who Have Been There Before You

There's no point trying to reinvent the wheel when numerous people before you walked that path. Find the right resources, gain from their success stories, and learn from their mistakes. Find a mentor or a coach to make your journey easier.

Today, Google is a good source of information on personal development and other transformational topics. Be curious and have a continuous learner's mindset. That's the price to pay if you want to get to where you want to be.

4. Embrace Change

Everything is bound to change. Whether you like it or not, change is inevitable. For example, your body is changing every day as you age. You can only slow the process, but you cannot stop it. Keep the anticipated change in mind, but don't make it your main focus. Embrace every progress you make toward your objective. Enjoy every step that brings you closer to your goal, and celebrate. Just know that the world we live in is the result of change initiative from people's ideas, and those same ideas are being renewed constantly. There is no escaping it. That's what makes up life.

Your personal self-development plan needs to include the new you that you want to see, and the actions you will take. Only action leads to results.

5. Be Accountable to Yourself

You are responsible for your own progress. You are responsible for *what* you are today and *where* you are today. That means it's your job to initiate the steps involved in your personal development plan. If you don't bother, no one else will. It also means that you own the results, and no one else is to blame. The buck stops here!

Focus on what you already have. Think about how others benefit from what you do. If you improve yourself, those benefits will increase. Your personal development is for others as well as for you.

6. Be Intentional

Whatever you intend, becomes your reality. Find your true intention before you resolve to do something, and make sure you really want what you say you want. If your goal and your intention are not aligned, then you'll think up lots of excuses and all sorts of situations to prevent your progress.

7. Challenge Yourself

Your goals need to be just out of reach. If you reach for an impossible target, you're setting yourself up for a failure. If you stick to what's easy, you're denying yourself the satisfaction of achievement, and only minimal change will occur. Find that middle ground with a stretch goal in your personal self-development.

8. Follow Your Passion

It's no good doing things that you don't like. Choose actions that appeal to you and are in line with your values.

Pick people to help you, whom you like being around. Make sure you're following your heart while not running from the hard issues. Become a master in the art of living, where people can't tell if you're working or playing because, to you, you're always doing both!

9. Keep Pressing Forward

Life works in cycles and moves to a rhythm. You will have ups and downs. When you hit a slow point, or things don't seem to be moving, don't give up; keep going. There is no such thing as continual rapid advancement, and that means your personal development plan needs to be achievable and balanced. Find your rhythm, and go with the flow. There's no such thing as finished personal self-development. You can go on learning, changing, and renewing for all of your life.

https://www.charlestchoreret.com/

*"Don't aim at success.
The more you aim at it and make it a target,
the more you are going to miss it.
For success, like happiness, cannot be pursued;
it must ensue, and it only does so
as the unintended side effect of one's personal
dedication to a cause greater than oneself."
– Viktor Frankl*

Chapter 8

Never Give Up

*"Most of the important things in the world have been accomplished by people who have kept on trying **when there seemed to be no hope at all.**"*
— Dale Carnegie

Achieving greatness is something that is hard to define. As an individual, it is your personal journey. What is it that distinguishes you from others in your field? What is it that makes you unique, and for which you know you can improve on and take to the next level?

What will help you manifest your best version is your personal idea on how you perceive greatness. There are, however, concrete ways for you to get started on achieving your dream of manifesting and expressing the best you in everything you do, and to be successful. Achieving a goal is a wildly exhilarating thing. If you're contemplating the idea of giving up, you could be throwing away the greatest opportunity of your life — your *best* future.

Lay your ground work to greatness, one step at a time, never giving up. Remember that the greatest obstacle to your progress is yourself. Never give in to the limiting voice inside of you, telling you that you are not good enough, the task is too great, or your ambition is overly great compared to who you are in terms of competence and qualification. That is fear, and F.E.A.R.—**F**alse **E**vidence **A**ppearing **R**eal—can stop you in your stride, rob you of your dreams, and steal your happiness.

Yes, there will be challenges. Why? Because life is not easy; there will be mountains to climb and challenges standing in your way, whether you like it or not. As a result, there's going to be anxiety, uncertainty, and fear about failing. No matter what happens, push yourself to keep going. After all, you'll never know how close you are to succeeding if you quit now. Therefore, you have to keep trying, no matter how tough it is. That's the price you need to pay before you complete the race.

"There is no failure except in no longer trying."
– Elbert Hubbard

Success in life is not reserved for a privileged few. We all have the capacity to unleash our greatness in whichever field we want to. Unfortunately, too many people are allowing their God-given gifts to remain dormant inside of them.

> *"Every day, people settle for less they deserve. They are only partially living, or at best living a partial life. Every human being has the potential for greatness."*
> – Bo Bennett

Let's be clear; greatness is, in my opinion, the highest level of satisfaction in personal accomplishment. It is a notion that resonates deeper than success; success being the tip of the iceberg (i.e. what people see, such as your possessions, your achievements, and what I have qualified as the glitter of life, which serves as the basis used by people to evaluate how successful you are).

Greatness, on the other hand, is the invisible part of the iceberg. It is made up of your God-given talents, which are manifested in everything you do. Greatness is not this esoteric, illusive, God-like feature that only the elite or the special among us will attain. Greatness is a God-given gift for every single one of us. All that is required of us is to tap into that gift so that it becomes the expression of everything we do while on this planet, by positively impacting the lives of others.

Have you ever asked yourself what your God-given abilities are? Let me tell the story of Moses, from the Bible. This is a typical example of how we as human beings don't realize the wealth of possibilities within is. All we need to do is tap into them and get the results we want.

When it was time for the Jews to be freed from Egypt, God spoke to Moses at the burning bush. He told him to go back to Egypt and lead the people out to the Promised Land. At that very moment, Moses lost his composure and started coming up with a flurry of justifications; something that most of us do when faced with a challenging task. Like Moses, we say or think to ourselves things like: "You've got to be kidding; I'm not the person for a job like that; I don't have what it takes; etc."

In Moses' case, God assured him that he would prepare the way, and that he would provide some pretty convincing miracles. Still, Moses had a hard time believing that he was up to the task. He pleaded: "I can't speak well; I don't have a college degree; I'm a convicted felon—please, send anyone else!"

Does this story resonate with you? You are given an obvious opportunity to grow, to be the leader you always wanted to be; yet you stall when the opportunity is presented to you. Wouldn't you like God to lay out such a clear plan for you, and to promise success in advance? I would. Wouldn't you want a coach or a mentor to give you a clear road map to your success, and to go step by step with you? Isn't that good enough for you?

In the case of Moses, it was not. He kept trying to convince God that he didn't have any of the necessary requirements for accomplishing this big job. Moses said, "They won't believe me. I don't have anything to qualify me for doing something great." God said, **"What is that in your hand?"** If you don't remember, it was his shepherd's staff, which turned out to be a pretty significant part of his leadership. He turned it into a snake, parted the Red Sea with it, and did some other pretty cool stuff.

If you think you're stuck, don't have any unusual talents, don't have the right degrees, and don't have the credibility to have people take you seriously, let me ask you a question: **"What do you have in your hand?"** What natural talents do you have? What is it that you do with excellence? Do you make beautiful candles? Delicious bread? Are you a talented speaker? Are you a good writer? Are you good at social work? Do you handle your children with grace? You get the idea—just look at what you have right in front of you, and capitalize on it to unleash the greatest you. With the right help, you may already have everything you need for greatness. Don't balk when you hear your call!

There is a race marked out for you; all you have to do is equip yourself with everything you need to start it and finish it well. To achieve greatness is a step-by-step process. It's more like a marathon than a sprint. As you cover each mile, you will discover more and more about yourself, and this discovery process will follow you all the days of your life, providing that you remain a fervent seeker of the best you.

You are like a long-distance runner who requires training, endurance, and discipline. You need to run the race marked out for you—a race driven by your God-given power(s). Stay on track and keep pressing forward, because there is no end to greatness, contrary to success, which can be limited and sometimes short-lived, and based on external circumstances. Greatness is a gift from the Universe—infinite, timeless, limitless, and abundant. If it was not so, it would be like limiting the Universe's ability to bless you abundantly.

Never Give Up

The power of the Universe cannot be put in a box, and since greatness is of divine intervention, it can never be limited. It is your responsibility to tap into what has already been given to you, and to strive. Start laying your bricks today, one brick at a time, and soon you'll have a tall and solid wall. The time to walk into your greatness is now. Believe that you can, do what is required, and you will.

Conclusion

Although we are coming to the end of our journey together, I have no doubt that through this book, in a way, we'll still be in touch. In the meantime, remember that greatness is about being intentionally focused on your personal development by equipping yourself with what is required to become the best version of yourself, and manifesting that new you in your interactions with people around you, and having a positive impact on their lives.

Being of service to others, and adding value to them, is the most rewarding satisfaction one can feel. It is a lasting one that will set you apart, not for selfish reasons but for reasons surpassing your personal interest. People you help will become your glory, your joy, and your success. The most influential people are the ones who leave incredible legacies behind, and they live on in the hearts of the people they've touched. Their principles, philosophies, and achievements become immortal, spreading from generation to generation. That is greatness.

Recently, I was watching a live video of Les Brown, on Facebook, where he discussed about leaving a legacy. He specifically said: *"I believe it is time for me to step back and train full time."* Like he said, his decision came about when he meditated one day on this existential question from **Leo Tolstoy**: *"As I face inevitable death, what in the purpose and meaning of my life will not be undone or destroyed when I'm gone?"*

Les Brown is one of the top five motivational speakers in the world. He has impacted the lives of over two billion people around the world for the past 50 years, and he believes that it's time for him to focus 100% on his health, so that he can still be around and healthy at 100 years old and beyond (he is 75 years old as I complete this book), enjoy the company of his children and grandchildren, and dedicate the rest of his life to training the next generation of speakers.

Despite all his speaking achievements over the years, he believes that he has not done his best work yet. According to him, his best work is to train even more speakers, so that the influx of people that he influences and touches, and the people that they in turn will influence and touch, shall not be interrupted. He wants to plant a seed that will outlive him.

Conclusion

What I take away from Mr. Brown's story is that achieving greatness in life is about passing on the baton by blessing others with your God-given gifts, and giving them a chance to spread their wings and strive.

What will be your legacy? How will you be remembered?

Your legacy will be forged based on the appreciation people have of your actions and how you impacted them.

Although I have come to the end of my journey with you, every time you open this book and use it as a reference on your path, I will be there with you.

Applying what I teach in this book is already a good part of the journey covered. However, the pursuit of greatness is an ongoing and sometimes bumpy road. No matter the challenges you may face, press on. At the end, everything will be all right; and if to this point, you feel that it is not all right, it simply means that it is not the end yet. Just keep on going, and keep on shining the greatest *you* that you can along the way. For every milestone, for every success, be your number one fan. Feel comfortable to congratulate yourself and to celebrate every achievement.

https://www.charlestchoreret.com/

Greatness is a continuous journey. Use the content of this book as the GPS to lead you to "the best *you* ever" destination, always showcasing the new persona you have become.

From now on, look at yourself in a different way: a bright, radiant, game changer; an entrepreneur, or whatever else constitutes your personal journey to greatness. Be that individual who is no longer driven by fear but rather by the newly built spirit of love, service, and abundance.

> *"True leadership and greatness*
> *are achieved not by reducing people*
> *to one's service, but in giving oneself*
> *in selfless service to them."*
> – Oswald Sanders

Thank you for allowing me into your life and for letting me guide you on your way to greatness.

To the greatest *you* always.

Conclusion

We can stay in touch via these platforms:

    Website: www.charlestchoreret.com
    Instagram: https://bit.ly/30gQCxk
    Facebook: https://bit.ly/3byICvj
    YouTube: https://bit.ly/33WSjB7

www.ingramcontent.com/pod-product-compliance
Lightning Source LLC
Chambersburg PA
CBHW070928160426
43193CB00011B/1613